MW00397980

More Advance P

## SALAMAT SA INTERSECTIONALITY

"Dani Putney's collection SALAMAT SA INTERSECTIONALITY shapeshifts ecstatic queer fire and blood through transformation, connection, and vibrant love. This is naming of experience that can't and won't hold still, because *you are a poem that breathes* or *Come sit in my vehicle while I issue you a warning* or *We don't have time. Your wife*. What an exhilarating debut, fast with adventure, deep with reflection, and sharp with theoretical barbs!" – Lisa Lewis, author of BURNED HOUSE WITH SWIMMING POOL and THE BODY DOUBLE

"The debut publication of SALAMAT SA INTERSECTIONALITY heralds a dynamic new voice in American poetry, a voice that can encompass themes as important and seemingly disparate as video games, classical piano, and gender identity, as elemental as nature, dive bars, and pickup trucks. These brave and vital poems confront and celebrate America as they crisscross the West, glorying in its light and landscapes, while challenging its intolerance and prejudice. In language equally at home in theory and slang, Dani Putney takes their speaker on a journey of self-discovery, coming into their own as a non-binary poet and citizen of the world. Buy this book. It will become your longtime friend." – Kendall Dunkelberg, author of A WRITER'S CRAFT: MULTI-GENRE CREATIVE WRITING and BARRIER ISLAND SUITE

"In their debut collection, SALAMAT SA INTERSECTIONALITY, Dani Putney kicks down your door to announce they have arrived. With familiars of scorpions, rattlesnakes, and bees, Putney sets fire to all boundaries as they navigate multiple identities in the harsh desert landscape of the American West. As I read this collection, I found myself unable to put it aside for fear that the pages were still burning behind me. Putney's language is as fearless as their subject matter: they move with craft and audacity through the intersections of tenderness and violence, violence and lust, lust and rage, rage and family, family and love. Read this book with a fire extinguisher in hand and a bucket of ice water at your feet." – Beth Gordon, author of MORNING WALK WITH DEAD POSSUM, BREAKFAST, AND PARALLEL UNIVERSE

"Dani Putney is an astounding poet of place. These poems teleport the reader to deserts, truck stop bathrooms, highway collisions—but also into moments of longing so realized they feel like a body being excavated. Poignant, unflinching, and powerful, SALAMAT SA INTERSECTIONALITY is an essential collection of poetry by a new and compelling queer voice. 'I want to live in the cracks of dry earth / outside *between* and *among* / where the queerest flowers grow.'" – Todd Dillard, author of WAYS WE VANISH

# Salamat sa Intersectionality

# Salamat sa Intersectionality

*Poems*

By Dani Putney

Okay Donkey Press

© 2021 Dani Putney

All rights reserved.

Printed in the United States of America.

Published by Okay Donkey Press

Los Angeles, CA 90034

www.okaydonkeymag.com

No part of this book may be used or reproduced in any manner without express written permission from the publisher except in the context of articles or reviews.

First Edition. May 2021.

ISBN: 978-1-7332441-5-2

Cover art: Sarah E. Shields

For Matt—if it weren't for you,
these words would still be
a lump in my throat


And for my mom,
mahal kita (yes,
that much)

I'm an unspeakable of the Oscar Wilde sort.

E. M. FORSTER, *MAURICE*

# Contents

## Mountain Coda

Dragon-breather, exhale across the great chasm,
burn my body into existence.
Sculpt me from dirt under your tail,
watch me materialize from dust.
Conjure earth fossa—your escarpment ally—
round my curves toward the tip of galaxy's thumb,
crack my bones into place.
Let valleys echo my spine,
lead coda one, two along thoracic vertebrae,
imbue my joints with musical Sierra.
Drown my baby lungs with snowmelt—
glacial cannibalism at its finest—
kill me as you fill me with mountain water.

Behold your work after final breath,
scoff for the wayward-leeward life you birthed,
do it again to create a better West.

# Youthful Absolution

Potato Bugs
*For Breanna*


Sitting on an electric box outside your house,
I told you potato bugs were tragically beautiful.
You mentioned wasps:
how an arrow lies on their striped abdomens,
nature's untouched codex.
There the poem started in your mouth—
a root canal to birth words.
Through circumstantial calculus
a beehive began to produce our honey.
Every good tree bears fruit,
like avocados on our late sandwiches,
decomposed into phosphorus and nitrogen.
We're cyclical:
time-chasers on this capitalist monument,
strings of marionettes dangling
our lines of dying light. Rooted,
you and I ink tragedy.

Sanctuary


You led me to an unexpected thicket.
We crossed a sagebrush-ridden ditch,
entered a window among the stems:

> I looked at the canopy,
> branches and leaves obscuring
> gray sky. Father's slurs—
> fairies and stick bundles—
> shed from my skin
> as detritus teardrops.

You walked me to your favorite
stump, wiped away my tears.
*We're in this together, Bug.*

> I hugged you, electric hair
> brushing my face, gauges tickling
> my cheek. I oozed
> in this embrace: our tiny forest
> caught in desert heat.

Nevada

A mustang was shot again,
northward where the desert glows,
mountain dreams flowing along the highway.
Guts decorate a thirsty earth,
flies battling, *It's my flesh, mine.*
If a horse is euthanized,
piled into a heap of horses,
does the energy recycle itself?
Blood can't beget nothingness,
can't re-create a wasteland
of diseased sand and Bureau of Land
Management conquerors whose bullets
carry the end. Sagebrush grows
where bones sink.

## To Judith Butler

If closet doors could speak,
they'd say *unravel*.
To festoon my body in silk is
to pick a scab     neurosis a style
never let the wound settle,
as in recovery     pre- and post-injury
or lava meant to freeze itself igneous.
The prickle of polyester
felt by a body in fashion
resists biological inertia:

>What's rest anyway
>but a prescription for gender,
>can't eczema on upper arms
>—hugging rolled sleeves—
>be enough?

The only tool Goddess gave us
was fascia,
language followed     then currency
then it made sense.
It's all relational     isn't it
the origin of commodities:

>Darwin, your beaks look like
>skin   hair   prick.

If closet epistemology burns cotton,
I was charred
before jumpsuits and rompers burst
—the criminologist found
pyrotechnic gossamer—

Pearls


It happens after *Mamma Mia!*
for the fifth time:

I place my cock in hand's pinhole grasp,
move back and forth
as fluorescent bathroom lightbulbs
let eyes process
brown skin on brown skin—

I try to conjure D cups bursting
from filigreed lingerie,
red lipstick stains trailing down my belly,

but all that comes is Colin Firth
dancing in his wet, pearly shirt

Gates of Paradise


Every time I say God,
you spit Leviticus.
My inner macabre

coaxes an apologist from me—
I'm sorry
for tainting your Bible

with marred skin, unholy saliva.
Forgive me, Mother,
for I have sinned.

Let me show you
the *Gates of Paradise*
at the Florence Baptistery.

Do you appreciate
gilded bronze,
perfect

linear perspective? How about
the ten Old Testament scenes
on each golden relief?

We'll walk through these doors,
I won't burst into flames—
don't hold my hand

to endow me with piety.
Heaven isn't
what you think it is.

# Shape

I sang my voicemail,
I was a diva those days,
      unformed as Earth
in its primordial years,
                 a soup
      teachers call it.
If ABBA taught me anything,
it was how to be a queen,
transcend myself and ride waves
of musicality,
         an essence unto itself.
*We need to talk,*
Father answered
—let me take off my shoes,
      too-large coat (I was even skinnier
      then)   *—Are you gay?*
not wasting time,
only concerned with truth, if
his theory was correct.
      The planet's a shaped mess,
happiness can't exist
in negative capability.  Who knew my body
         would remain    -less?

Memories of Sacramento


I want to know
how I felt watching
the frame's glass shatter,

pierce my brother's skin
like it was paper,
his wailing in pain,

blood pushing
through little hands
to stain the hallway carpet.

Ma cursed his negligence,
tears carved his cheeks,
my body remained still.

I need to know
why I didn't cry,
why I didn't tremble.

Lactose Intolerance

I call you Moo-ma
because you said I'd grow
into a big cow
if I drank my glass.
*You know the Buddhists worship them?*
I'll never forget
your Visayan hand on my shoulder,
circles rubbed into the blade
of my interstitial body.
*Don't rush it—*
you knew the milk I spat
wasn't a color
but a single white reflection
neither of us could escape.

When Dad shook his head at me,
I remembered:
*Your brothers grew tall.*
If I gulped the toxin,
smacked my lips to compliment
his American joy,
I could escape to the bathroom
and clutch a belly yellow
where white had seeped out.
I'd count the scars
along my intestines
where every glass cut me.

Moo-ma, look,
am I worthy of worship?

Father's Estate

Tell me about the blond man on the beach
with hairless chest and Pacific eyes.
I want to know why he's nestled
between photos of your first
two wives, your eight children.
If only you didn't go
to high school in the '50s,
tried not to listen
to jokes from your Air Force buddies.
If only your mom or dad or best friend
grabbed you by the cheeks, said,
*Your feelings are beautiful.*

        All I can do now is forgive:
        for your flotsam,
        your life nearly lived.

Dissociate


If I close my eyes
on I-80 for five seconds,
my body evaporates.
It floats above blacktop
as an observer of clockwork:

beast to metallic beast,
a grid of commuters and lovers
and travelers and murderers,
each individual patched
onto an unearthly mass.

The spirit drifts
farther away, a ghost
of a ghost. The body and car
careen into the adjacent river.
Before metal meets water—

Eureka

*you are a poem that breathes*:

they tell me but pick my skin
written in typeface—

bold, blotches of melanin stamped
on hands and feet like Black Death,

diseased by body, voice, confessional lungs,
midwifed by Plath,

her touch vibrating my bones, nerves
as each syllable drops

from finger to page,
ink spill coming, rubbing the squid dry,

my Courier gadget in the toolbox—
I breathe because I am, I am, I am,

my skin ripped and torn by them, by nature,
and I smile wide

because I am a poem that breathes

My Mom Was a Picture Bride


I fell into her stereotypically          Asian dress
cherry blossoms          Mandarin collar          slit skirt
        (later I'd hear cheongsam)
and my blood blossomed into a mango tree outside Manila:
                        each fruit a photograph
                        mailed to Golden Coast vets itch-
                ing, *the good years*
                                buried in brown pussy
        I was his bride
        middle-aged face above me
                wait-
                ing to be fucked
        womb filled with imperialism-turned-
        globalization          but I wanted it
                more than future children know
                more than parents who paid to place
                my body in American ads
I tell others
her cheongsam connects me
to my heritage
                though I mean
        it makes me feel pretty
        when I want to be bought
and if people are lucky I'll say
        the dress matches
        jade earrings my mom gave me
        when discover-
ing womanhood
beneath
        a half-boy

Filipinx


Ghosts swim across the Pacific,
say hello through my tap.
Outside Talisay City
water is polluted—
        human feces, urine
            from untreated septic tanks.
They came to warn me.

I also think they came
to bring me cancer.
Half my mother's siblings have died
from shapeless facial tumors.
She never bathed in the sea,
her parents knew the water
was never safe.

When I fear
the lump on my neck has      metastasized
I know I'm my mother's child.
Death by cell overgrowth
would mire me in ancestral love,
dispel earthly doubts
I was never Asian enough.

I wrap my mouth around the faucet,
        mix spirits with saliva,
            gulp years of heritage down my throat.

Toyland

1.
200-mile-per-hour airbags shot me
in Hazen, Nevada. The alt-rock song
playing on my speakers
devolved into garbled static,
my ears began to ring.
I swear I heard silence
within the chemical fog
suspended around the car seats.

I existed in a space between reality
and fiction, where I was dead
and alive inside a toy car on a toy highway.
It must have been sabotage,
whoever left that truck tire on the road.

2.
The welts on my arms healed quickly,
the tire disappeared quicker,
but I can still see the trail of antifreeze
and pieces of plastic skin
I left behind
in a ghost-town turnout.

## Math Class

I wanted him
to fuck
the calculus out of me
as I clawed
his gilded shoulder blades,
icicle eyes piercing
my flesh.

# Frogs

We descended into California
marshlands. Frogs lured us
from campfire reverie
with their pulsating ribbits.

Red Solo cups,
flashlights in hand,
we muddied our boots searching
for amphibian treasure.

First target:
a tiny leopard frog
resting, oblivious
to our coup.

We seized
the creature,
placed it in my cup.
Looking at vacuous black eyes,

I thought about the life
we intended to steal.
My friends laughed.
I dropped the cup.

# The High School Spelunker's Guidebook

*Verso*

Together we rappel cavern walls,
only backpacks and headgear
to claim, careful to avoid
guano-covered stalagmites
and whip scorpion nests.
We share the gleam of
*Courage!* in our eyes
as we see little but feel
dirt in our boots, dust
in our lungs. We're bats
in the fray, echoes carving paths
into our skin. We may die
2,000 feet under, but our blood
will fertilize the earth.

*Recto*

My blood will fertilize
the earth. I'll die 2,000 feet
under. You snap my cord,
kick me onto the tallest
stalagmite. My back breaks
as you etch laughter
into my synapses—this cavern
is yours. Whip scorpions
surround my failing body:
eviscerated bowels, sawtooth
vertebrae. My organs weep.
I want to curse your shadow,
but my throat vomits dust,
lips speak in forgotten dirt.

# Freedom in Six Parts

1.
I remember him
complaining about Spanish class.
Those were the days I mistook
youthfulness for absolution.

2.
¿Por qué no está en la cárcel?
He wore victimhood
like a war story,
convinced me the devil lives
in a woman's heart.
Pero es el diablo.

3.
His hands left holes all over—
skin the gun,
touch the bullet.
I let him burn you.

4.
Crime begets punishment,
only we're choked
by man's grip.
He thought himself
extraordinary.

5.
All I see is un monstruo.
Merriam-Webster gives this:
He faced a life sentence

on charges of rape.
If only a dictionary
could set us free.

6.
No estamos libres
mientras él está libre.

## Lost Boys

Our dirty feet stomp
around burning skin, around
eyeballs drooping from sockets, around
charred ears ready for supper.

We lock soot-stained arms as brothers,
pray to the moon.
Banshee keen scatters night creatures,
protects our sacred campfire.

Together we make the first cut.
Blade cleaves dinner's foot
from ankle—O boyhood,
we celebrate with flesh tonight.

# Salted Pores

Dissonance

I want to behold him
in nothing but boots and Cattleman,
sunburnt skin brined,
dirty-blond chest hair
reflected in porch light.
I want to lap salt off forearms,
chew scar-decorated shoulders,
tongue dead-celled neck.
I need to inhale grass
and dirt and dirt and dirt.

He doesn't need to talk—
I don't want to hear about
horses and guns and women.
I want him to shove me against
ranch-house stucco, rub
hardness into my soft
city mind. Our callused knuckles
speak a common language:
the wilderness,
the forgotten metropolis.

Desert Tango


You and I played monkey-wrenchers
as we passed yellow tractors
scattered around our dusty path.
We catapulted rocks at metallic beasts
like amateur saboteurs—
this desert was ours. But Abbey
didn't teach us sabotage,
we only wanted to be men
for each other.

Burnt soil captivated us
with its Pollock-esque facade.
We saw lavender in the rough
against subtle tonalities
of uprooted bedrock.
        Today, our memories
        are colors—blink—
we're a two-person gang again,
our skin whipped by sand.

Snails

When his tongue
slid across my teeth
I thought of escargot—
slime all over my incisors.
I wanted to swallow
its foreignness.

Outside,
lips were earthy
like his desert origins,
each chapped sliver of skin
a horseback ride
through sagebrush.
For thirty seconds
we were cowboys:
ranch house, kids,
barnyard sex.

He let go.

# Berm

Your pink palms stroke my face,
cheeks flush sanguine as you finger
bristles along my jawline.
Your tundra gaze, my throbbing
veins, punctuated by the aroma
of dewy grass, toxic to my lungs
like Marlboros that grace
your nether lip every twilight.
I bite, lap blood off
your chapped skin, plunge
my tongue into salivary nirvana.
*Do you like how you taste?* I think
but will not say, every breath
subtracts from our waltz.
I dare not close my eyes
as your hands traverse
my sweaty back, claw
stiff vertebrae. Exploding
pupils remind me
you crave this, too.
I foist my body
onto yours, roll with me,
bello, linen stains prove
we know our embrace.

## Call Me Wallaby

Tuck me into your fat,
nuzzle my cheek as I unravel
within your belly, escapee
of the prickly desert.
The microcosm of our macro-
molecular pouch births the bilayer
of sandwiched love, caught
in a furry blizzard of eyelash kisses,
tongue dances, umbilical matrimony.
We're hypodermic bygones,
tangled in a hop-hop interstice,
stitched to the convergent cells
of paws interlocked,
caked in dirt.

## Worknight Tango

He lounges on our gray recliner,
tungsten lamplight reflects his face.
Crow's feet smile—
revelations   mishaps
          non sequiturs—
thumb and index finger clasp
page bottom,
wrist muscles contract.
An intellectual.
I return my gaze
to paperwork splayed
                    across my desk.

His hand grasps
my shoulder, I take off
reading glasses, look at
a smirk and graying beard.
          *You're distracted.*
He grabs my hand,
takes us to our bedroom.

# Hyacinths

Bury me
  by the hyacinths
bumblebees play on.
  I picked them
at the nursery, you said
  they were beautiful
like me. Fill my pores
  with soil—I'll leave
you a garden.

They Call It "LGBT Family Building"


You squeeze my slick palm,
we walk into our first consultation.
I've never thought myself a sweaty person—
bless my mother's Southeast Asian genes—
*Don't worry*, you interject.
I weakly offer my thanks-
but-that-doesn't-fix-anything smile.
*We're just looking at our options*,
your lips graze. This kiss,
it makes me think I want to marry you,
even though you saw me frown
too many times at your friend's Big Fat
Irish Wedding, listened to me curse
assimilation during *Queer Eye* binges,
our legs entwined like couch sardines.

       Last night I prayed to a nameless creator,
       begged Them to make me infertile.
       50 percent chance of failure, I thought.


*You first, straight shooter.*
I hand you a checklist of pre-existing conditions.
Your eyes crack, not unlike
teary crows that flock
when you wrestle with favorite nephew
on our pit bull–trodden carpet,
erupt into action-figure Chautauquas,
gunfire and victory speeches,
succumb to requests to play video games,
*Pretty please, Uncle.*
We sign the patient consent form.

I'd rather become the alien in our home
than war with a phantom.

## Freudian Discontent Regarding Patterned Sexuality

We slipped into a foursome
in a truck-stop shower:
you, me, and the older mixed-race couple
from that French bistro in Portland.
The Latino with graying sideburns grabbed
my lapels, kissed me into the fading
seafoam wall tiles. I cupped his erection
outside raw denim jeans.
Fingers traveled southward
while he whispered *dámelo* in my ear.
Lightning.

Mid-fingering, I glanced at you blowing
my partner's white, respectable husband.
His eyes were closed behind foggy Ray-Bans,
hip thrusting steadily into your mouth.
I saw blood swelling your cheeks,
the way they used to be when we fucked.
Next to those wall tiles
you were radiant,
dare I say an angel in our tryst.
You've never looked so beautiful
with a dick in your mouth.

## Across the Desert

1.
Bees made their hive
above the attic window.
I asked you, *Can we keep it?*
*If it's not wasps*, you said.

2.
When I moved in, I insisted
we alphabetize our bookshelf
by first name, not last.
I told you it was ironic that
*Birthday Letters* touched *The Colossus*.
You shrugged and walked off.

3.
I cut my ring finger.
Sitting on our toilet seat, I watched
the blood form a perfect bead.
You handed me a bandage and flashed
that Hughes smile she and I used to love.
I thought about the bees.

4.
A year ago I crossed the desert
while you stood waiting
by the Oasis of Nevada.
I jokingly thought you were my savior,
Aryan neo-Nazi. Maybe
it was her guiding me.

5.
A bee near the backdoor
startled our dogs. You swatted it
with a handful of bills
and threw away the body.
I didn't have a chance
to ask about the hive.

6.
Sylvia, tell me,
should I leave here?

## Don't Freeze with Me

Freefalling from the railing
I close my eyes,
withdraw my hand from yours,
hope to die while your body
survives another scar.
Our car thuds against white earth
sprinkled with cones,
lodges itself in drift.
Blood pours from my forehead,
glass in eyelashes,
ulna through forearm tattoos.

My eyes remain shut
despite your screeches,
your mouth full of erupted teeth.
I can't look at your lacerated body,
tongue can't produce 9-1-1.
I sit deafblind in the driver's seat,
snowmelt mixing with bone and flesh,
hands screaming from airbag blisters.

I'll die obscured by the Sierra.
Conifers serve as final witness,
your howls inscribe my epitaph.
Let me freeze here
while the ambulance carries away
your blazing body.

Mantis

A tiny kiss behind the ear:
all it takes to make a grown man

melt. I live in locker-
room whispers,

blow death kisses
to passersby. Brother

to Lamia, we're partners
in heart-devouring.

*A powerful creature,*
I've been told.

# Texas Tango

Midday, I-40, about 80 miles east
of Amarillo. Pink asphalt, cracked.
A ditch of half-dead grass. My Kia,
straddling humanity and nature.
His SUV, all red-blue lights
behind me. *Better slow down,*
passing drivers must think.
He approaches my window.
*Come sit in my vehicle while I issue
you a warning*, he says. I get out
without thinking. I'm walking. *No,
this can't be right*, my mind
catches up. *I don't feel comfortable
getting in your car*, I blurt out.
*You're not the only one to be
apprehensive*, he replies. He points
at a cheap patch on his upper arm:
*Highway Patrol*. His blond hair,
thinning. His eyes, a blizzard.
*Why am I walking toward his
passenger-side door?* HP logo,
weathered. Black paint, chipped.
An echo: *This can't be right.*
Drivers passing by: *Must be serious.*
I clutch the door's handle
with a sweaty palm. I know myself.
I'm afraid of what I want.
His window, rolled down. I see him
across a tundra of upholstery.
Top button, undone, chest hair
creeping out of his shirt. I think of

my dad. I get in. *My name is Dean,*
he tells me. The scene, set.

Salt

*Stop at The Matador,*
*the best dive New Mexico's hiding.*

Indigo walls littered with frames greet me,
men in biker jackets and torn jeans don't.
*Can I get a G&T?*
I ask the tatted, beanie-clad bartender.
Everybody's staring—
they know I don't belong,
pink dress shirt and floral blazer don't fit.
I hand the bartender my card, but he points
to a pinned-up shrine of Johnny.
*Cash only*, he deadpans.

Before I open my mouth,
a fleece pullover and baseball cap says,
*I got it.* I spurt out
*Thank you*, reach for my phone.
*What's your name?* he asks.
I know what he wants—
his lips, the icicles
of his unwavering gaze,
I've seen it before.
*I have to go to the bathroom.*
He knows I know.
I follow him because damn it,
I want it, too.

He swaggers into a red door:
a graffitied excuse for a restroom.
*Whatever you are, be a good one,*

45

a sign above the toilet instructs.
Again, I play teacher,
helping middle-aged men relearn pleasure
like boys discovering masturbation.
They want to be touched *here* and *there*.
I kneel, this stranger's *sweet boy*.
He unbuckles, unzips.
Salt fills pregnant pores
softly, sharply.

# Introduction to Literary Theory and Criticism

In our face-to-face meeting
he was bold:
peeling a banana, inserting
the phallus into his mouth.
Suit and tie, pomaded hair,
conveniently delayed lunch—
he must've waited for me.
*Let's talk about your writing,*
his words slid off crooked teeth.

After our queer theory unit
he said his sexuality was
*expanding*, an experiment
in disentanglement. Derrida taught us
deferral of meaning—here,
mid-afternoon, his closet of an office,
tongue laced with potassium.
My essay critiquing *Mulan*'s
Americanized Chinese iconography
was appetizer to soft brown hair,
freckles along his forearms.

*Lean in, inhale*
*his banana breath,*
my thoughts instructed. No need
to convince this pretty boy.
I became the other students—
we've all heard tales—
            take me out, stroke my hand,
            the next part is easy.
            Command my flesh like young scholars
            budding into intersectional feminists.

Lazarus

I follow him
to his mama's abandoned trailer.
*American Gothic* shudders
around us, our jeans fade like sky
excavated from sunflower soil.

We arrive among weeds.
He teeters
before shifting boots,
rubbing tan-orange arms
bedecked with freckles.

On a dusty futon
his eyes gut me:
a boy wilting again.
I remember all
the women he's mentioned.

He unbuckles, eases off
denim. A speck of urine
rests on frayed cotton
—I breathe deep.

Lessons in Sculpture

His shoulder blades shift
against a taut shirt
to create a concavity

toward the small
of his broad back.
Cargo shorts exhibit rugged legs,

a gleam shimmering from his calves—
he must be a hiker or a cyclist
or a god.

His arms rest evenly at his sides,
forming a void
between torso and forearm.

The window frames of shoulder to thumb
highlight his virility,
outlining each finger, knuckle, wrist, elbow

against Nevada sun.
I see pieces of boyish adventure
in the trail of blond hairs

that descend his neck.
I think:
pillow forts, treehouses, desert expeditions.

His mother must be proud of him,
her little rabble-rouser. She must have
his wife already picked out.

## Advanced Studies

The baby-blue fabric of his dress shirt reaches past my waist. I
feel like a child in his hotel room. He's in the shower, door
slightly cracked, steam escaping. He's singing AC/DC, I think
"Thunderstruck." *Rock these days ain't like the classics*, he told
me last night. I walk to the kitchen—I've never been in a hotel
room with a kitchen. I grab the carton of eggs he bought us,
remembering, *I always love an omelet the morning after*.
They're brown, I think they're supposed to be healthier. They
remind me of his face: crow's feet, forehead wrinkles. I crack an
egg on the edge of a skillet, move to turn on the stove—
somebody's holding my waist. *Hey*, he whispers, his tongue
sliding down my neck. My hands relax, I ease into his kiss. I
smell his Irish Spring body wash: All men must smell like this.
It's like he's tucking me in. But I stop. *We don't have time. Your
wife*. I push his hands off. He pouts, returns to the bathroom. I
turn on the stove, cook his egg.

Dollhouse

He called me his "little bird"
and patted my head
every time I argued,
*I want to see you more*
*than every other weekend.*

He clenched his jaw
yelling into the phone
every time coworkers were "imbeciles"
and interrupted his weekends with me.

He said he loved me
after sex and a cigarette,
but every time we fucked
he looked at himself in the mirror,
never embraced me.

He showed me pictures of his dog,
a Golden Retriever.
Every time I asked to see his family,
he growled, "Stop asking."

He told his friends
I was his cousin
every time he brought me in public.
I thought, never said,
*It's not normal to fuck your cousin.*

He left me the day his wife
got pregnant.
Every time he makes love to her,
does he look in the mirror?

Jouissance


My body is a grave
        where I'm reborn
        as god   (dess)  of pleasure.
I want him inside me.     I want to become him.
        My body trembles
            as his hand glides along my spine.
I lean into     callused palm—worker's touch—
hardness alive with memories
of power tools   lumber   too much dirt.
I tongue sweat off his digits,
think about the holes     spelunked.
My DNA forges
            a cosmos of possibility
                within his pores,
connected by touch,
master   master   *master me*
            *please*
excavate and refill over     and over.

# Taken Root

Western Mythology
*For Matthew Shepard*


2 by 2, hands of dirt,
they grapple my shoulders from behind.
Cowboy sweat slips into my slashes, burns,
our stenches mingle to form sarsaparilla death.
No. 1 laps blood off my ear,
carves a river across deflated chest,
whispers, *You like that, queer?*
His pal lifts a cigarette from dry lips,
rubs it *real good* into my wrist,
cackles in tune to hyena brothers, sisters
who love to devour meat like me.

2 by 2, their hands force my head
into spikes 3: mouth, cheek, eye yolk.
Face next to barbed wire,
I smell rust, taste enamel dislodged,
sliced through tongue, gums, empty sockets.
Fluid leaks from punctured sclera,
sight becomes oblivion,
hot breath crawls down my neck.
*Tie him up, make it tight.*

2 by 2, boots clack
against gravel, shadows enter
their pickup. The engine screeches alive,
headlights, I speak your language:
*Take me to purgatory*—rush, sweep,
the truck targets my wilting flesh,
I hear black.

Scar

is my favorite Disney villain:
a matriarch in his step,
moths netted in his throat.
Stare into those corrosive irises,
half-shuttered as in high,
it's like killing a patriarch's son
has psychoactive properties.
I've always seen myself
in his brother's blood—or,
I knew I was evil
well before Father called me
*fag*. Thank you, Disney.

If villainy were simple,
I'd peel off my face
and celebrate violence
as art itself: The king is dead,
long live the charming prince.
But *simple* doesn't mean
*beautiful*, as in the angularity
of Scar's mane, the soft
masculinity of his undulating
torso—pieces to adorn
my lion body. Evil is in style,
so call me a killer.

## A Token Isn't Worth Anything

I fasten a donkey button onto my chest
—I'm trapped:
        At the campaign gala,
        clumps of invective-stuffed dirt
        rupture my taste buds.
        Politicos and I condemn elephants
        outside the room, celebrate
        my colorful DNA with fine
        wine glasses, toast to shared freedom.
        But men's kindness is a mythical fuel,
        powered by super PACs,
        poured into their pseudo-
        Democratic mouths. I'm their flag,
        brandished by suit after suit
        who will never know the touch
        of another man. I hope
        their corporate walls crumble
        to expose rainbow-blinded zombies
—take my guts,
savor the taste.

# Sylvia Plath and Virginia Woolf Talk on My Thighs

I ask them:
Did you want to be inked
behind a shadowbox of leg hair?
They respond with a kiss
across my thigh gap
and I say a thigh gap isn't feminist
but they say *hush, darling,*
*your twink body has never been so free,*
*its kaleidoscope is buried in your skin.*
　　　　*Excavate it.*
Heather Love taught me to feel backward
but I'm unstuck.
I ask:
How do I become a woman?
　　　　*Nothing.*
How do I become a man?
　　　　*Nothing.*
I say guwapa
they say
　　　　*mabuhay*
I say guwapo
they say
　　　　*mabuhay.*
I'm waterborne across the delta
　　　　　　　　of my
　　　　　　　　　gender—
did I transcend flesh to become a goddess?
No, the queerest part of me is
black leg hair upon Cebuano skin,
curves splitting a tight waist,
hands with hairy knuckles and bony knuckles
and the softest knuckles anyone knew.

## Cybernetic Impromptu

Call me Chopin,
these hands span octaves.
Not my own digits, or are they,
attached to wrists
the diameter of Neverland bracelets,
Pan style, could be delayed
development. Little finger to thumb,
I stretch ten, men comfortably
reach nine, am I man now,
I promise I'll care for these electric

digits. Youth for grace
notes, knuckle hair for steel
bones. No, manufacturers use titanium,
prosthesis equals indestructible feathers,
body growth tangled with gravity.
Chopin's heart knew tension well,
I his hands—mine now—one to ten,
A to C. I must be boy made into
man, I must be an-      droid,
I must be.

## If They Equals You

When I die,
I know they won't
call me by my name.
They'll use a legal designation
with a   third person   I outgrew.
Can I mourn my inevitable   erasure?
Or rather: Don't tell me
            death is any sweeter.
There can't be release
if my fascia was never   connected
to their social organism,
            a multicellular façade.
But I knew that—
                  absence   isn't erasable.
Every part of a cell is important,
down to the   space   in between.
I should ask:
What do I feel
   when I'm nothing to mourn,
      when my cells don't contain
      the interstitial jelly called presence?
(I can't capitalize my presence
                  if it doesn't exist.)
*He was loved*, they'll say.

# A Practical Guide to Confronting Racism

I can't take my eyes off:
You clasp a chilled Coors Light,
shuffle Ariat boots,
adjust your rodeo hat.
The woman to your left tells a story,
maybe about her day at work,
maybe about nothing at all.
Your crush is obvious despite
the flames in my eyes,
the bonfire between us,
the smoke engulfing my brain.

It's possible she doesn't know
what you're hiding behind
a hazel gaze and one-step-above-
peach-fuzz on your upper lip:
> *Confederate flag waves*
> *from your old pickup,*
> *slurs bark—windows down—*
> *as desert donuts bake,*
> *an unquestioning pal*
> *howling in the passenger seat.*

I stride past partygoers,
make a beeline to your
compensation-times-five truck,
navigate to the rear tire.
I piss, steam rising
from unexpected warmth,
moon's penumbra my witness.
I cackle, marvel

as abominable mixed DNA decorates
your American-made chick magnet.

## Imago

Team-building activity:
anonymously submit
your greatest fear.
I think about lying,
everybody loves
a predictable untruth.
Hail Mary, I scribble
the word on a scrap,
place folded sheet
into circulating box.

*Incest.*      Frown.
*Who thought*
*it would be funny*
*to write such a thing?*
*Take this      seriously.*
I nod, look down
at my hands—
            they were a boy's once, untouched—
hope nobody mistakes
tremors for guilt.

I listen to
heights, spiders, the ocean,
excuse myself, *My stomach is upset.*
I race to metallic home,
            sterile stalls, lineup of mirrors,
can't make it, vomit
            erupts,
for a second
I'm happy.   Release.

Less bile means less
flesh, means I'm closer
to a skeletal physique.
If I shed myself,
I can be rid
of the memory
of his touch,
my pupa can realize
        imago.

My mirrored gaze
betrays me, reminds me
he lives within.
On cynical days I think
it's all Freudian,
his hands on me
the reason I have a daddy
complex, why fantasies of sweat
mixed with leather excite me.
        Mostly I have nightmares.
I can't remember
how it felt,
sometimes I don't remember
it happened.

        *Mirror, please tell me*
                *I didn't like it.*

## OCD

You'll break the lamp
on your desk and use the shards
to stab a colleague.

So you move the lamp
to the corner of your desk.
A colleague will pass,
you'll slam their face
into the lamp, glass on purple lips,
what a mess.

So you bury the lamp
under your desk, nothing to see.
You'll unscrew the bulb,
thumb your way to the filament,
rub the readymade shark's mouth
along your leg. *What's that
crackling sound?* a colleague will ask.

So you smash the lamp
in the parking lot, fragments airborne
like sand in medias res.
No more lamp, unless
you buy another on sale at Target,
put it on your desk tomorrow.
*What a pretty lamp*,
a colleague will say.

You'll break the lamp.

## Stuck in Primordial Soup

*Cogito.*
I wake up, put on a body:
Business Formal Male,
bowtie     cufflinks     Oxfords.
I look in the mirror,
see another Lacan.

*Ergo.*
Routine:
a body abused by the elements
—capital and capital and capital—
the linear function of time,
O normative worker, O perpetual commute.

*Sum.*
I want to exchange this body,
remove flesh from my closet.
Years of evolution
but sweat under fat rolls
smells of     apocalypse.

PDX Queen

If I say I'm a poet
I become a relic.
If I say I'm trans
my body becomes ars poetica.
TSA says
*Good morning, ma'am*
       but tells me
       *Have a good day, sir.*
Am I immune to the agent's scrunched-
up face because they want
          to get it right?
That agent should know
nothing feels right,
don't punish yourself.
If pages wept
every time a stranger
blew butterflies in my face
       —sculpted me in their binary image—
I'd have too many poems.
This world has too many poems,
not enough queens—
not enough borderlands to germinate
               queenliness.
        I want to live in the cracks of dry earth
    outside *between* and    *among*
where the queerest flowers grow.

# Michelangelo

was a twink. Have you seen
Adam, his nude reflection, reach
for Father's hand like a boy
needing touch? I've lain on my own
Renaissance bed, the sinews
of arms and legs awaiting
transformation into a father
I wished I had. Maybe it's a lust
for the impossible: manhood.
I spent my youth with Italian artists
frolicking across my amygdala—
yearned for a beauty within paintings
produced by twinks condemned
to homoerotic chastity.
I cover my body in art
to remind myself of this evolution,
that flesh exists in conversation
with emotional memory, a co-
habitation of past and future.
You see, all my bones give
is neutrality: I was never born
to become Dad or Mom
or the transition from one
to the next. Let me be
the sculpture I'm creating.

## Angeligender

the online quiz assigns
after I select
    a. robes with cosmic energy;
      b. color of the universe; and
        c. mercenary of God.
Rarest of demiboy, a-
gender, biogender, I always knew
I was different, barely

human. Sometimes I joke
I'm a male-bodied spirit—
how did the test calculate
    my incorpo-
            real coexistence?
I don't mind a flat chest
and leg hair. I'm a sculpture
animated with angel wings,
can't you see them? Their gossamer
flows around us.    I kid.

I'm told identity
equals flesh, not other-
kin. Reality is    —but
the truest I've felt was in   nothing,
by which I mean
my body is a vessel for   everything.
I'm melting from unmade gods.

Repping in the *Borderlands*


Character selection:
    magical slum woman,
    ex-assassin à la Irish grandpa,
    mech-loving soldier lady,
      or robot beastmaster.
It's obvious: no better way
to blaze across moon rocks
and galaxy's-edge conflict zones
than as a gentlethemly AI
built to slay. In a universe where
mayhem equals fun, the he/she
of humans matters even less
than good vs. evil. Too many inter-
stellar bounties to pick anything
besides self:
      I loot space as a they/them
      non-human.
A choice to other players is a flare
signaling my return home.
Even with video-game classics
like androgynous Link and baby-pink
Kirby, I've never felt as close
to an assemblage of pixels—or,
I've never known joy like ignoring
a white man and two women to select
the me I didn't know existed.
And boy, doesn't it feel right to pistol-
whip alien desperados, my pronouns
on their bleeding tongues,
my metal vibrating with the hunt.

## Dear Jeremy

I sucked your dick,
then you became a Mormon.
Is this identity retrograde
or reaffirmation of a truth
you tried to flee,
my tongue the escape rope?
Sometimes all we are
is latent heteronormativity.

What I'm trying to say:
I want you to remember me
at inconvenient times like mid-
coitus with your Utahn wife
or in the shower alone
with your thoughts + hands.

What I really mean:
I hope I didn't turn you off
to Raphaelite beauty,
discourage you from the allure
of humanity's androgyny—
if I'm not beautiful,
what am I? What gets me
by is queer narcissism, a love
of replicating myself
through those around me.

I can't understand
why you married a window
rather than a mirror, why
your reflection of me
wasn't enough.

## 150 Years of Molt

I come alive in the dirt between my toes.
Minerals of high-desert sand tell me
stories of mountaintops and wastelands from far ago.
Breaths of summer air dizzy me,
the sun of the heartland burns my flesh.
I can't see except for the brown of my skin,
the brown of my dirt.

The trail at my feet, in my blood,
leads me to the ancients.
I feel archaeologists rediscover me
as I'm lured into the Great Basin.
I toss stones—my weathered toys,
pet sagebrush—my faithful pet.
Calluses, scratches on my hands
remind me why I'm here:

This land has consumed me,
thrown me into the dirt.
Every bite of a fire ant, rattle of a snake
petrifies my bones. I become
stalactites among the caves,
petroglyphs on the rocks.
Dry heat liquefies my Pacific coast,
replaces it with minerals at my feet.
I'm the desert taken root.

## Parasitism

It lands on my knee
to say the wave
is coming     but it's only
a boxelder bug so I flick
—no no lover
          time to dance—
and the screen door rips cross
-wise w/ lumberjack force,
a red swarm charges.
The insects grapple my chest hair
like pirates kissing the coastline
but rougher     mouth parts scratch
-ing, they're biting, I think
I love it as a boy loves
his daddy     bears gone wild
on my skin, inside organs
as Octavia Butler's "Bloodchild"
—am I pregnant? yes yes
          to the flesh I'm growing,
earth's little warriors parasitized
my lungs into splendor     or maybe
gave me an ovipositor
to dangle below a hairy crack,
     don't deny how much you lust it,
they telepath—     and they're right
to assume this invasion was
anything less than wanted.

## Post-apocalyptic

1.
I wake among eviscerated liver-kidney-rectum,
wipe eyes with bloody knuckles,
smile for the bile of yesterday's
survival. Another romp
through our queer hellscape.

2.
My body thrives in our world's transition
from falling apart to long gone—
I'm the interstice,
the guy or gal in Prada combat boots
and one-piece death dress.

3.
The infected come, come, cum
as I chop through necklines,
splatter Z-positive gunk on limb-ridden beds.
My comrades—partners in flux—
laugh at our slaughterhouse.

4.
Agender Ray and androgynous Jay
don't know the power of our wasteland.
I want to twist and shout every time
we kill among ruins of before:
a corporate reproduction.

5.
Comrades become
frozen fingertips and unshaven faces:

O barely anything lives,
we own ourselves.

Salamat sa Intersectionality


I'm not growing into a Man
under indigo sky, on saffron fields.
My swamp hemolymph perspires through Cebuano skin:
thick and brown, pliable and brown.
Manure-rich air depresses my joints,
supple as the wrist-flicks of white Man signatures
of 1776, of iced black –not green– tea, of Ben Franklin orgies.

I'm not patriotically un-Man,
just orient-ally brown, un-human.
My teeth are whiter than mold that dampens
my carcass, litter on a saffron field under indigo sky.
What remains is gelatinous scat
mixed with cow pats +
Bud Light + Cattleman.

I'm not the pioneer un-Woman
or the Cebuana manic pixie dream girl.
My closest relative is Kafka's monster—
we bleed kaleidoscopes, scare cow(Men), repel suburbia.
Our faces don't read West-East, M-F.
Man buries us in mud, smiles,
says *God bless America.*

# Memento Mori

I see a crumpled SUV
at the foot of the mudslide.
Its bumper grimaces
like a chrome parabola.
Two ambulances slow down
ahead of me as I look
at tiny drops of rain
pummeling my windshield—

> *Tart mush*
> *of Prozac on my tongue,*
> *empty bottle at my feet,*
> *Dad pleaded,*
> *"Don't do it, don't do it"*—

EMTs approach the SUV
in my rearview mirror,
rain slackens to a drizzle.
I place a hand
over my heart, remembering
its resonant timbre.

Convergent Boundary
*For Cody*


It's always a mountain
 — through me into
 you, or is it simply
  *us*, as in the glacier
 that carved our initials
 across this valley  —
take me back, I want
yarrow on my fingertips
again, like your pollen, like
my blush under starlight,
I know you've looked,
precious, it doesn't take
metaphor to recognize
the dazzle of *we*
 — through you into
 me, is this geology
  yet (an adverb meaning
 perfect), we were frozen
 then but taste of dirt
  now, I swear another
 word for time is
 petrichor  —
cyclical, rain on yarrow,
or valley's flush, I didn't
mean to write a science
lesson, but if we began
on a mountain, our through-
way to love is convergence
 — take me back.

## Sidewind into the Universe

Standing atop Rattlesnake Hill,
the sun slashes
        my cheek.
Skin peels
off, melts down
my thighs     slithers
toward a puddle of gravel.
Wind catches my molt,
fertilizes the hillside.
     *Crescendo.*
Earth brought me here
to witness
my undoing,
        my becoming.
Quarks buzz my limbs,
xylophone to the cosmos:
     *Coda.*
        *Coda.*

# Notes

The phrase "lines of dying light" in "Potato Bugs" pays homage to Dylan Thomas' poem "Do not go gentle into that good night" (1951).

"Nevada" was inspired by William Brewer's poem "West Virginia," included in his collection I KNOW YOUR KIND (2017).

"To Judith Butler" is a response to Butler's 1992 interview with Liz Kotz for the international art magazine *Artforum*.

The opening line in "Eureka" comes from the header on largerloves.tumblr.com. Additionally, the phrase "I am, I am, I am" in this poem pays homage to Sylvia Plath's novel, THE BELL JAR (1963).

"Lost Boys" was inspired by William Golding's novel LORD OF THE FLIES (1954).

"Berm" was inspired by André Aciman's novel CALL ME BY YOUR NAME (2007).

"Dollhouse," including the use of the term "little bird," was inspired by Henrik Ibsen's play A DOLL'S HOUSE (1879).

"Jouissance," specifically the title and the line "My body is a grave," was inspired by scholar Leo Bersani's article "Is the Rectum a Grave?" (1987).

"Western Mythology" offers a fictionalized account of Matthew Shepard's brutal murder. Shepard was a gay University of Wyoming student tortured, set on fire, and left to die in the freezing cold in a remote area near Laramie. Some accounts say his face was covered in blood except for the areas cleansed by tears.

The line "Heather Love taught me to feel backward" in the poem "Sylvia Plath and Virginia Woolf Talk on My Thighs" is a reference to Love's book FEELING BACKWARD: LOSS AND THE POLITICS OF QUEER HISTORY (2007).

"Cybernetic Impromptu" considers Polish composer Frédéric Chopin's large handspan. More information about Chopin's memorable hands can be found within this 2014 *Atlas Obscura* article by Allison Meier: atlasobscura.com/articles/objects-of-intrigue-chopins-hand.

The lines "I look in the mirror, / see another Lacan" reference psychoanalyst Jacques Lacan's concept of the mirror stage, or when an infant recognizes themselves in a mirror and, therefore, as an external object.

"Angeligender" was inspired by the non-binary gender quiz at uquiz.com/quiz/JTSkiB/which-non-binary-gender-are-you. The answers (a., b., and c.) listed in this poem include verbiage from the quiz.

"Post-apocalyptic" was originally written as a queer reimagining of T. S. Eliot's poem "The Waste Land" (1922) but has since evolved into its present form.

"Convergent Boundary" was named after the geological area where two or more tectonic plates collide. The collision of these plates is one way mountains are formed. More information about tectonic plates, convergent boundaries, and mountain formation can be found within the digital library TeachEngineering: teachengineering.org/lessons/view/cub_rock_lesson04.

# Acknowledgments

Thank you to the following journals and magazines for first publishing these poems, most in earlier forms:

*#EnbyLife*: "Dissociate," "Lazarus," "Stuck in Primordial Soup"

*Alien Magazine*: "Dear Jeremy"

*The Blue Mountain Review*: "Hyacinths"

*Brushfire Literature & Arts*: "150 Years of Molt," "Across the Desert" (as "Revelation Across the Desert"), "Dollhouse," "Freudian Discontent Regarding Patterned Sexuality," "Lessons in Sculpture," "Pearls," "Western Mythology" (as "Marsha P. Johnson Threw the First Brick")

*Camas*: "Repping in the *Borderlands*" (as "Representation in the *Borderlands*")

Cathexis Northwest Press: "Post-apocalyptic," "Salamat sa Intersectionality" (as "Salamat for Intersectionality"), "They Call It 'LGBT Family Building'"

*The Chaffin Journal*: "Father's Estate" (as "Father Gone"), "Memories of Sacramento"

*Cosmonauts Avenue*: "If They Equals You," "Scar"

*detritus*: "Lost Boys," "Math Class"

*Elephants Never*: "A Practical Guide to Confronting Racism"

*Empty Mirror*: "Freedom in Six Parts," "Gates of Paradise," "Potato Bugs"

*Feminist Spaces*: "A Token Isn't Worth Anything"

*FERAL: A Journal of Poetry and Art*: "The High School Spelunker's Guidebook" (as "The Spelunker's Adventure Book")

*Foothill*: "Imago," "My Mom Was a Picture Bride"

Ghost City Press, *My Loves*: "Berm"

*Ghost City Review*: "Sanctuary"

*Glass: A Journal of Poetry*: "Lactose Intolerance" (as "Milk")

*Juke Joint Magazine*: "Filipinx," "Shape"

*LandLocked*: "Angeligender," "Michelangelo"

*Lockjaw Magazine*: "Call Me Wallaby," "Jouissance," "Sylvia Plath and Virginia Woolf Talk on My Thighs," "To Judith Butler"

*Loose Leaf*: "Toyland"

*Marías at Sampaguitas*: "Memento Mori"

*The Matador Review*: "Introduction to Literary Theory and Criticism"

*Mojave Heart Review*: "Nevada"

*Mura*: "Advanced Studies," "Desert Tango" (as "Desert Play Date")

*Noble / Gas Qtrly*: "Mountain Coda" (as "Born on the Mountainside")

*Page & Spine*: "Eureka" (as "Poet")

*Prismatica Magazine*: "Mantis," "Parasitism"

Qommunicate Publishing, *Queer Around the World Too*: "PDX Queen" (as "PDX Tote Bag Aesthetic and New Year's Eve Expectations")

*Random Sample Review*: "Texas Tango"

*The Shore*: "Sidewind into the Universe"

*Sons and Daughters*: "Worknight Tango"

*Thin Air Magazine*: "Convergent Boundary," "Cybernetic Impromptu," "OCD"

*trampset*: "Dissonance"

*Transcend*: "Salt"

*Tule Review*: "Don't Freeze with Me"

*Vamp Cat Magazine*: "Frogs," "Snails"

Thank you to Okay Donkey Press, especially Genevieve Kersten and Matt Broaddus, for believing in this collection. I'm thrilled that my reflections on being a quadruply minoritized desert dweller struck a chord with you!

Thank you to my graduate professors Kendall Dunkelberg, Brandy Wilson, and L. Lamar Wilson for providing invaluable feedback on these poems. This collection exists because of the various ways they've shaped and unraveled its constituent pieces.

Thank you to my MFA cohort, especially Lilyanne Kane, Pietje Kobus, Xenia Sylvia Dylag Murtaugh, Carrie Penrod, Tracy Pitts, Lauren Rhoades, C. T. Salazar, Randi Sanders, and Celeste Maria Schueler. All their suggestions live in these poems. Plus, I'm endlessly grateful for our shared revelry in Mississippi, Portland, and San Antonio.

Thank you to my best friend, Breanna Inga, and to Rebekah M. Devine, my partner in literary crime, for critiquing many of these poems. I couldn't have made it this far without them.

And thank you to my partner, Cody Sammons, for supporting my creative writing, even though I know he thinks I'm an insufferable poet. Thanks for letting me bring up literary theory during dinner conversations and wax philosophical before bed. I love you, old man.

# About the Author

Dani Putney is a queer, non-binary, mixed-race Filipinx, and neurodivergent writer originally from Sacramento, California. Their poems appear in outlets such as *Empty Mirror*, *Ghost City Review*, *Glass: A Journal of Poetry*, *Juke Joint Magazine*, and *trampset*, among others, while their personal essays can be found in journals such as *Cold Mountain Review* and *Glassworks Magazine*, among others. They received their MFA in Creative Writing from Mississippi University for Women. While not always (physically) there, they permanently reside in the middle of the Nevada desert. SALAMAT SA INTERSECTIONALITY is their debut poetry collection.

Also Available from Okay Donkey Press

GHOSTS OF YOU by Cathy Ulrich
WAYS WE VANISH by Todd Dillard
DEATH, DESIRE, AND OTHER DESTINATIONS
by Tara Isabel Zambrano

Made in the USA
Monee, IL
14 May 2021

67503213R00069